Y0-BYW-596

This journal belongs to

....

BOARDING PASS

NAME

Tyle

9

Dopra
hl.
Metra, El.
Jizden
ve st
jednu
mést
oopra
Dopra
hlavni

34

You are an amazing child of God, precious to Him in every way.
As you seek Him, He will show you the mysteries of life and unfold
His unique plans for you—a life full of rich blessings and delight.

Wherever your journey may take you, God is right there
with you. He is as close as breathing. Let this journal inspire
you to express your thoughts, embrace your dreams,
record your prayers, and listen to what God is saying to you.

For the LORD your God will be with you wherever you go.

JOSHUA 1:9 NIV

TRAVEL POCKET JOURNAL

BOARDING PA

NAME   FLIGHT NO

FROM

SEAT NO

Ellie Claire

gift & paper expressions

...inspired by life

1. to go from one place to another, as by car, train, plane, or ship; take a trip; journey 2. to travel,

pass through or over, as a country or road. 3. to journey or traverse to distant places.

travel \trav•el\

CONVERSION CHARTS

WEIGHT

1 ounce = 28.3 grams
1 gram = 0.035 ounce
1 pound = 0.454 kilogram
1 kilogram = 2.2 pounds

VOLUME

1 pint = 0.473 liter
1 liter = 1.76 pints
1 quart = 0.95 liters
1 liter = 1.05 quarts
1 gallon = 3.79 liters

LENGTH/DISTANCE

1 inch = 2.54 centimeters
1 centimeter = 0.394 inch
1 foot = 0.3 meter
1 meter = 3.28 feet
1 mile = 1.61 kilometers
1 kilometer = 0.62 mile

TEMPERATURE

°F	°C
104	40
100	38
86	30
68	20
59	15
50	10
41	5
32	0
-40	-40

Simple formulas for
converting temperature:
$(C \times 2) + 30 = F$
$(F-32) / 2 = C$

Open your mouth and taste, open your eyes and see—
how good God is. Blessed are you who run to him.

PSALM 34:8 MSG

....

....

....

....

....

....

....

....

....

....

....

....

....

....

....

I have wandered all my life, and I have traveled; the difference between the two is this—we wander for distraction, but we travel for fulfillment.

HILAIRE BELLOC

You see me when I travel and when I rest at home.
You know everything I do.

Psalm 139:3 NLT

To travel hopefully is a better thing than to arrive.

ROBERT LOUIS STEVENSON

Walk in the paths [God] shows you...then you'll
get on well in whatever you do and wherever you go.

1 KINGS 2:3-4 MSG

9

Each of us may be sure that if God sends us on stony paths
He will provide us with strong shoes.

ALEXANDER MACLAREN

You will show me the path of life;
in Your presence is fullness of joy.

PSALM 16:11 NKJV

Savor little glimpses of God's goodness and His majesty, thankful for the gift of them: pathways through the woods, a bright green canopy overhead, and dappled sunshine falling all around.

Honor and majesty are before Him;
strength and beauty are in His sanctuary.

PSALM 96:6 NKJV

9

....

....

....

....

....

....

....

....

....

....

....

....

....

....

Do not follow where the path may lead. Go instead where there is no path and leave a trail.

T. S. ELIOT

I am guiding you in the way of wisdom,
and I am leading you on the right path.

PROVERBS 4:11 NCV

....

....

....

....

....

....

....

....

....

....

....

....

....

....

In order to see where we are going, we not only must remember where we have been, but we must understand where we have been.

ELLA BAKER

All you need to remember is that God will never let you down...
he'll always be there to help you.

I CORINTHIANS 10:13 MSG

9

Two roads diverged in a wood, and I—I took the one less traveled by, and that has made all the difference.

ROBERT FROST

Small is the gate and narrow the road that leads to life, and only a few find it.

MATTHEW 7:14 NIV

Our days are identical suitcases—all the same size—but some people can pack more into them than others.

Teach us to number our days aright, that we may gain a heart of wisdom.

PSALM 90:12 NIV

9

He who does not get fun and enjoyment out of every day
needs to reorganize his life.

GEORGE M. ADAMS

When people's steps follow the LORD,
God is pleased with their ways.

PSALM 37:23 NCV

....

....

....

....

....

....

....

....

....

....

....

....

....

....

Security is mostly a superstition. It does not exist in nature....
Life is either a daring adventure or nothing.

HELEN KELLER

God, who got you started in this spiritual adventure, shares with us the life of his Son and our Master Jesus.

I CORINTHIANS 1:9 MSG

9

Remember, no matter where you go, there you are.

EARL MAC RAUCH

I am with you and will watch over you wherever you go.

GENESIS 28:15 NIV

If people concentrated on the really important things in life, there'd be a shortage of fishing poles.

DOUG LARSON

Look at the birds, free and unfettered, not tied down to a job description, careless in the care of God. And you count far more to him than birds.

MATTHEW 6:25-26 MSG

Adventure is worthwhile in itself.

AMELIA EARHART

Surely your goodness and unfailing love will pursue me all the days of my life.

PSALM 23:6 NLT

The longer I live, the more my mind dwells upon the beauty and the wonder of the world.

JOHN BURROUGHS

Your life is a journey you must travel
with a deep consciousness of God.

I PETER 1:18 MSG

There will stretch out before you an ever-lengthening, ever-ascending, ever-improving path.... But this, far from discouraging, only adds to the joy and glory of the climb.

Sir Winston Churchill

We have been greatly encouraged...dear brothers and sisters,
because you have remained strong in your faith.

1 THESSALONIANS 3:7 NLT

Little acts of kindness...in everyday life are like flowers by the way-side to the traveler: they serve to gladden the heart and relieve the tedium of life's journey.

EUNICE BATHRICK

If your gift is to encourage others, be encouraging.
If it is giving, give generously.... And if you have
a gift for showing kindness to others, do it gladly.

ROMANS 12:8 NLT

....

....

....

....

....

....

9

....

....

....

....

....

....

....

....

Nature has been for me, for as long as I can remember,
a source of solace, inspiration, adventure, and delight.

LORRAINE ANDERSON

Everything God created is good, and to be received with thanks....
God's Word and our prayers make every item in creation holy.

I TIMOTHY 4:4-5 MSG

A new path lies before us; we're not sure where it leads;
but God goes on before us, providing all our needs.

LINDA MAURICE

> Trust in the Lord with all your heart, and lean not on your own understanding; in all your ways acknowledge Him, and He shall direct your paths.
>
> PROVERBS 3:5-6 NKJV

9

Dopr
hl
Jizden
ve sr
jednu
mest
dopra
Dopra
hlave

3,4

9
6
3

B O A R D I N G

NAME   FLIGHT NO

FROM   TO

You have to allow a certain amount of time in which you are doing nothing in order to have things occur to you, to let your mind think.

MORTIMER J. ADLER

Whatever is true, whatever is noble, whatever is right, whatever is pure, whatever is lovely, whatever is admirable—if anything is excellent or praiseworthy—think about such things.

PHILIPPIANS 4:8 NIV

At every crossroad, follow your dream. It is courageous
to let your heart lead the way.

THOMAS LELAND

My aim is to raise hopes by pointing the way to life without end.
This is the life God promised long ago—and he doesn't break promises!

9

When preparing to travel, lay out all your clothes and all your money.
Then take half the clothes and twice the money.

SUSAN HELLER

Steep your life in God-reality, God-initiative, God-provisions.
Don't worry about missing out. You'll find all your
everyday human concerns will be met.

MATTHEW 6:33 MSG

Take a chance! All life is a chance. The person who goes furthest is generally the one who is willing to do and dare.

DALE CARNEGIE

Use every chance you have for doing good.

EPHESIANS 5:16 NCV

9

Life...gives you the chance to love and to work
and to play and to look up at the stars.

HENRY VAN DYKE

The heavens declare the glory of God, and the skies announce what his hands have made. Day after day they tell the story; night after night they tell it again.

PSALM 19:1-2 NCV

God wanted to join us on the road, to listen to our story, and to help us realize that we are not walking in circles but moving toward the house of peace and joy.

HENRI J. M. NOUWEN

Live in me. Make your home in me just as I do in you.

JOHN 15:4 MSG

9

Think of whatever you are doing as an adventure and watch your life change for the better.

WILFERD A. PETERSON

Embracing what God does for you is the best thing you can do for him....
Fix your attention on God. You'll be changed from the inside out.

ROMANS 12:1-2 MSG

One cannot collect all the beautiful shells on the beach. One can collect only a few, and they are more beautiful if they are few.

ANNE MORROW LINDBERGH

How precious to me are your thoughts, O God!
How vast is the sum of them!
Were I to count them, they would outnumber the grains of sand.

PSALM 139:17–18 NIV

....

....

....

....

....

....

....

....

....

....

....

....

....

....

When I look back at where I've been, I see that what I am becoming is a whole lot further down the road from where I was.

GLORIA GAITHER

God is gently calling you...to an open place of freedom
where he has set your table full of the best food.

Job 36:16 NCV

In the long run, the pessimist may be proved to be right, but the optimist has a better time on the trip.

DANIEL L. REARDON

Put your hope in the LORD. Travel steadily along his path.

PSALM 37:34 NLT

9

Dopr
h
l´stre, E
Jizdo
ve st
jednu
měst
dopra
Dopr
hlav

3,4

9
6
3

Discoveries are often made by...going off the main road,
by trying the untried.

FRANK TYGER

Dear friend, listen well to my words.... Those who discover these words live, really live; body and soul, they're bursting with health.

PROVERBS 4:20, 22 MSG

The most important trip you may take in life is meeting people halfway.

HENRY BOYE

Encourage each other. Live in harmony and peace.
Then the God of love and peace will be with you.

2 CORINTHIANS 13:11 NLT

Every now and then go away, have a little relaxation. For when you come back to your work, your judgment will be surer.

LEONARDO DA VINCI

The instructions of the LORD are perfect, reviving the soul....
The commands of the LORD are clear, giving insight for living.

PSALM 19:7-8 NLT

They travel lightly whom God's grace carries.

THOMAS À KEMPIS

GOD, your God, carried you as a father carries his child.

DEUTERONOMY 1:29 MSG

What we call the end is also a beginning.
The end is where we start from.

T. S. ELIOT

He has planted eternity in the human heart, but even so, people cannot see the whole scope of God's work from beginning to end.

ECCLESIASTES 3:11 NLT

Certainly, travel is more than the seeing of sights; it is a change that goes on, deep and permanent, in the ideas of living.

MIRIAM BEARD

Knowing what is right is like deep water in the heart;
a wise person draws from the well within.

PROVERBS 20:5 MSG

May the road rise to meet you, may the wind be always at your back....
And, until we meet again, may God hold you in the palm of His hand.

IRISH BLESSING

The LORD bless you, and keep you; the LORD make
His face shine on you, and be gracious to you.

NUMBERS 6:24-25 NASB

The really happy person is one who can enjoy
the scenery on a detour.

The signposts of God are clear and point out the right road.
The life-maps of God are right, showing the way to joy.

9

Today is your day! Your mountain is waiting. So...get on your way.

THEODOR SEUSS GEISEL (DR. SEUSS)

Come, let us go up to the mountain of the LORD.... There he
will teach us his ways, and we will walk in his paths.

ISAIAH 2:3 NLT

....

....

....

....

....

....

....

....

....

....

....

....

....

....

I can't decide where I want to go until I know where I am.

True to your word, you let me catch my breath
and send me in the right direction.

PSALM 23:3 MSG

9

You'll learn more about a road by traveling it than by consulting all the maps in the world.

Show me the right path, O Lord; point out the road for me to follow.

PSALM 25:4 NLT

An adventure is only an inconvenience rightly considered.
An inconvenience is only an adventure wrongly considered.

G. K. CHESTERTON

At the end of the journey we'll surely rest with God.
So let's keep at it and eventually arrive at the place of rest.

HEBREWS 4:10-11 MSG

....

....

....

....

....

9

....

....

....

....

....

....

....

....

....

Life is not a journey to the grave with the intention of arriving safely... but to skid across the line broadside, thoroughly used up, worn out, leaking oil, shouting *Geronimo*!

BILL MCKENNA

Do you not know that in a race all the runners run, but only one gets the prize? Run in such a way as to get the prize.

1 CORINTHIANS 9:24 NIV

God will not send us out on any journey for which He does not equip us well.

ALEXANDER MACLAREN

My God shall supply all your need according to
His riches in glory by Christ Jesus.

PHILIPPIANS 4:19 NKJV

9

....

....

....

....

....

....

....

....

....

....

....

....

....

....

A good friend is a connection to life—a tie to the past,
a road to the future, the key to sanity in a totally insane world.

LOIS WYSE

There is a friend who sticks closer than a brother.

There is no pleasure in having nothing to do; the fun is in having lots to do and not doing it.

MARY WILSON LITTLE

What I'm trying to do here is to get you to relax, to not be so preoccupied with *getting*, so you can respond to God's *giving*.

MATTHEW 6:32 MSG

9

Dopra
hl.
Maire. El.
Jizdenk
ve stro
jednu
mésto
dopra
Dopra
hlavni

34

9
6
3

Life begins each morning.... Each morning is the open door to a new world—new vistas, new aims, new tryings.

LEIGH MITCHELL HODGES

The faithful love of the LORD never ends! His mercies never cease. Great is his faithfulness; his mercies begin afresh each morning.

LAMENTATIONS 3:22-23 NLT

Meeting someone for the first time is like going on a treasure hunt.
What wonderful worlds we can find in others!

EDWARD E. FORD

I have not stopped giving thanks to God for you.
I always remember you in my prayers.

EPHESIANS 1:16 NCV

9

God invites *you* to vacation in His splendor. He invites *you* to feel the touch of His hand. He invites *you* to feast at His table. He wants to spend time with *you*.

MAX LUCADO

The glory of GOD—let it last forever! Let GOD enjoy his creation!

PSALM 104:31 MSG

....

....

....

....

....

....

....

....

....

....

....

....

....

....

I would like to travel light on this journey of life, to get rid of the encumbrances I acquire each day.... I come to be only as I lose myself.

MADELEINE L'ENGLE

I'll stride freely through wide open spaces as I look
for your truth and your wisdom.

PSALM 119:45 MSG

9

....

....

....

....

....

....

....

....

....

....

....

....

....

....

The use of traveling is to regulate imagination by reality, and instead of thinking how things may be, to see them as they are.

SAMUEL JOHNSON

Blessed are those who have not seen and yet have believed.

JOHN 20:29 NIV

Rest is not idleness, and to lie sometimes on the grass under the trees on a summer's day, listening to the murmur of water...is by no means a waste of time.

SIR JOHN LUBBOCK

The Lord is my shepherd; I shall not want. He makes me to lie down in green pastures; He leads me beside the still waters.

PSALM 23:1-2 NKJV

98

Dopra
hl.
Šairn, El.
Jizdenl
ve stro
jednul
mést
doprav
Doprav
hlavní

3.4

9
6
3

BOARDING

NAME   FLIGHT NO
FROM   TO

Isn't it splendid to think of all the things there are to find out about?
It just makes me feel glad to be alive—it's such an interesting world.

LUCY MAUD MONTGOMERY

God is wise in heart and mighty in strength.... He does great things past finding out, yes, wonders without number.

JOB 9:4, 10 NKJV

God has promised strength for the day, rest for the labor, light for the way, grace for the trials, help from above, unfailing sympathy, undying love.

ANNIE JOHNSON FLINT

Go in peace. The presence of the LORD
be with you on your way.

JUDGES 18:6 NKJV

9

Time you enjoyed wasting is not wasted time.

T. S. ELIOT

My soul finds rest in God alone; my salvation comes from him.

PSALM 62:1 NIV

It is God to whom and with whom we travel, and while He is the end of our journey, He is also at every stopping place.

ELISABETH ELLIOT

The LORD himself goes before you and will be with you;
he will never leave you nor forsake you.

DEUTERONOMY 31:8 NIV

9

We are not alone on our journey. The God of love...sent us His only Son to be with us at all times and in all places, so that we never have to feel lost.

HENRI J. M. NOUWEN

God loved the world so much that he gave his one and only Son so that whoever believes in him may not be lost, but have eternal life.

JOHN 3:16 NCV

For the pathway that lies before me, my heavenly Father knows—
I'll trust Him to unfold the moments just as He unfolds the rose.

My foot has held fast to His path;
I have kept His way and not turned aside.

. . . .

. . . .

. . . .

. . . .

. . . .

. . . .

. . . .

. . . .

. . . .

. . . .

. . . .

. . . .

. . . .

We may run, walk, stumble, drive, or fly, but let us never lose sight of the reason for the journey, or miss a chance to see a rainbow on the way.

GLORIA GAITHER

My child, don't lose sight of common sense and discernment.
Hang on to them, for they will refresh your soul.

PROVERBS 3:21-22 NLT

Our road will be smooth and untroubled no matter what care life may send; if we travel the pathway together, and walk side by side with a friend.

HENRY VAN DYKE

Make every effort to keep yourselves united in the Spirit,
binding yourselves together with peace.

EPHESIANS 4:3 NLT

Though I have seen the oceans and mountains, though I have read great books and seen great works of art...there is nothing greater or more beautiful than those people I love.

CHRISTOPHER DE VINCK

May the Lord make your love for one another and for all people grow and overflow, just as our love for you overflows.

1 THESSALONIANS 3:12 NLT

God puts each fresh morning, each new chance of life,
into our hands as a gift to see what
we will do with it.

May God give you more and more grace and peace as you grow in your knowledge of God and Jesus our Lord.

2 PETER 1:2 NLT

9

Life is what we are alive to.... Be alive to...goodness, kindness, purity, love, history, poetry, music, flowers, stars, God, and eternal hope.

MALTBIE D. BABCOCK

May our Lord Jesus Christ himself and God our Father...encourage your hearts and strengthen you in every good deed and word.

2 THESSALONIANS 2:16-17 NIV

When you're traveling, you are what you are right there and then. People don't have your past to hold against you. No yesterdays on the road.

WILLIAM LEWIS TROGDON

We grow like a flower in the field. After the wind blows, the flower is gone, and there is no sign of where it was. But the LORD's love...continues forever and ever.

PSALM 103:15-17 NCV

9

F_{or} all of us, whether we walk old paths or blaze new trails, friends remain important.

LOIS WYSE

Two are better than one, because they have a good return for
their work: If one falls down, his friend can help him up.

ECCLESIASTES 4:9-10 NIV

No one realizes how beautiful it is to travel until he comes
home and rests his head on his old, familiar pillow.

LIN YUTANG

> Come to me, all of you who are tired and have
> heavy loads, and I will give you rest.

MATTHEW 11:28 NCV

9

There will always be the unknown. There will always be the unprovable. But faith confronts those frontiers with a thrilling leap. Then life becomes vibrant with adventure!

ROBERT SCHULLER

By faith we understand that the entire universe was formed at God's command, that what we now see did not come from anything that can be seen.

HEBREWS 11:3 NLT

Every day is an opportunity to make a new happy ending.
May you live all the days of your life.

JONATHAN SWIFT

Love GOD, your God. Walk in his ways...so that you will live, really live, live exuberantly, blessed by GOD.

DEUTERONOMY 30:16 MSG

May your footsteps set you upon a lifetime journey of love.
May you wake each day with His blessings and sleep each night in
His keeping. And may you always walk in His tender care.

Stand at the crossroads and look...ask where the good way is, and walk in it, and you will find rest for your souls.

JEREMIAH 6:16 NIV

Don't hurry, don't worry. You're only here for a short visit so be sure to smell the flowers along the way.

WALTER HAGEN

I run in the path of Your commands,
for You have set my heart free.

PSALM 119:32 NIV

9

Though we travel the world over to find the beautiful,
we must carry it with us or we find it not.

RALPH WALDO EMERSON

I am with you and will watch over you wherever you go.

GENESIS 28:15 NIV

For my part, I travel not to go anywhere, but to go.
I travel for travel's sake.

ROBERT LOUIS STEVENSON

Your life is a journey you must travel with
a deep consciousness of God.

I PETER 1:18 MSG

Walk on a rainbow trail; walk on a trail of song, and all about you will be beauty. There is a way out of every dark mist, over a rainbow trail.

NAVAJO SONG

I set My rainbow in the cloud, and it shall be for the sign of the covenant between Me and the earth.

GENESIS 9:13 NKJV

Friendship brings people close no matter how great the distance between them.

The amazing grace of the Master, Jesus Christ, the extravagant love of God, the intimate friendship of the Holy Spirit, be with all of you.

2 CORINTHIANS 13:14 MSG

....

....

....

....

....

....

....

....

....

....

....

....

....

....

Around me when I look, His handiwork I see;
This world is like a picture book to teach His love to me.

JANE E. LEESON

For since the creation of the world God's invisible qualities—
His eternal power and divine nature—have been clearly seen.

ROMANS 1:20 NIV

L ike all great travelers, I have seen more than I remember, and remember more than I have seen.

BENJAMIN DISRAELI

Light is sweet, and it pleases the eyes to see the sun.
However many years a man may live, let him enjoy them all.

ECCLESIASTES 11:7-8 NIV

God give me joy in the tasks that press,
in the memories that burn and bless;
In the thought that life has love to spend,
in the faith that God's at journey's end.

THOMAS CURTIS CLARK

Work hard and serve the Lord enthusiastically. Rejoice in our confident hope. Be patient in trouble, and keep on praying.... Always be eager to practice hospitality.

ROMANS 12:11-13 NLT

TRAVEL POCKET JOURNAL

© 2011 Ellie Claire™ Gift and Paper Corp.

www.ellieclaire.com

Compiled by Barbara Farmer

Cover and interior design Jeff and Lisa Franke

All rights reserved. No part of this book may be reproduced in any form
without permission in writing from the publisher.

Scripture references are from the following sources: The Holy Bible, New International
Version®, NIV®. Copyright © 1973, 1978, 1984 by Biblica, Inc.™ Used by permission of Zondervan.
All rights reserved worldwide. The New King James Version (NKJV). Copyright © 1982 by
Thomas Nelson, Inc. Used by permission. The New American Standard Bible® (NASB),
Copyright © 1960, 1962, 1963, 1968, 1971, 1972, 1973, 1975, 1977, 1995 by The Lockman Foundation.
Used by permission. The Holy Bible, New Living Translation (NLT), copyright 1996, 2004.
Used by permission of Tyndale House Publishers, Inc., Wheaton, Illinois. *The Message* (MSG).
Copyright © 1993, 1994, 1995, 1996, 2000, 2001, 2002 by Eugene Peterson. Used by permission
of NavPress, Colorado Springs, CO. The New Century Version® (NCV). Copyright
© 1987, 1988, 1991 by Thomas Nelson, Inc. Used by permission. All rights reserved.

Excluding Scripture verses and divine pronouns, in some quotations references to
men and masculine pronouns have been replaced with gender-neutral references.

ISBN 978-1-60936-163-1

Printed in China